SARAH'S SECRET
90 DAY POCKET PLANNER

Copyright 2016 ~ FunSchoolingBooks.com

Sarah's **SECRET** Message is on the Last Page! Shhh... Keep it a secret.

Name:

Date:

Email:

Phone#:

Address:

HOW TO GET OUT OF SURVIVAL MODE:

You can't do it all,
but you can do a lot.

You have big dreams,
and your life is so demanding.

Maybe you wonder how
you will ever
accomplish anything important.

HERE'S THE PLAN:

Do FOUR important things
every day for 90 days.
If you skip a day, just begin again!

If you write down your four goals every morning,
or every night before you go to bed, you might
actually change your life, live your dreams,
and get out of survival mode.

Start Today.
Turn the Page!

DAY 1

Date:_____

Choose **FOUR** <u>important</u> things
that you can accomplish today.

Reflect on Yesterday's Accomplishments:

_____
_____
_____

DAY 2

Date:_____

Choose **FOUR** <u>necessary</u> things that you can accomplish today.

My Dreams for Tomorrow:

_____
_____
_____

DAY 3

Date:_____

Choose **FOUR** <u>important</u> things that you can accomplish today.

Reflect on Yesterday's Accomplishments:

_____
_____
_____

DAY 4

Date:_____

Choose **FOUR** <u>necessary</u> things
that you can accomplish today.

My Dreams for Tomorrow:

DAY 5

Date:_____

Choose **FOUR** <u>important</u> things
that you can accomplish today.

Reflect on Yesterday's Accomplishments:

_____
_____
_____

DAY 6

Date:_____

Choose **FOUR** <u>necessary</u> things that you can accomplish today.

My Dreams for Tomorrow:

DAY 7

Date:_____

Choose **FOUR** <u>important</u> things that you can accomplish today.

Reflect on Yesterday's Accomplishments:

_____
_____
_____

DAY 8

Date:_____

Choose **FOUR** <u>necessary</u> things
that you can accomplish today.

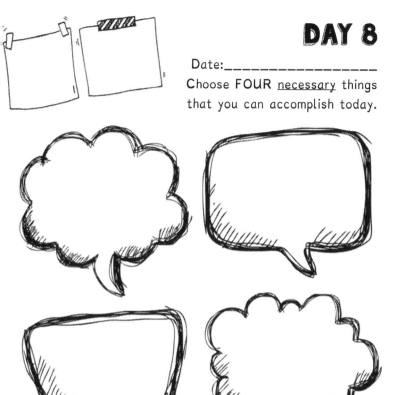

My Dreams for Tomorrow:

_____
_____
_____

DAY 9

Date:_____

Choose **FOUR** <u>important</u> things
that you can accomplish today.

Reflect on Yesterday's Accomplishments:

_____
_____
_____

DAY 10

Date:_____

Choose **FOUR** <u>necessary</u> things
that you can accomplish today.

My Dreams for Tomorrow:

_____
_____
_____

DAY 11

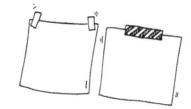

Date:_____

Choose **FOUR** <u>important</u> things
that you can accomplish today.

Reflect on Yesterday's Accomplishments:

_____
_____
_____

DAY 12

Date:_____

Choose **FOUR** <u>necessary</u> things that you can accomplish today.

My Dreams for Tomorrow:

_____
_____
_____

DAY 13

Date:_____

Choose **FOUR** <u>important</u> things that you can accomplish today.

Reflect on Yesterday's Accomplishments:

DAY 14

Date:_____

Choose **FOUR** <u>necessary</u> things
that you can accomplish today.

My Dreams for Tomorrow:

_____
_____
_____

DAY 15

Date:_____

Choose **FOUR** <u>important</u> things
that you can accomplish today.

Reflect on Yesterday's Accomplishments:

_____
_____
_____

DAY 16

Date:_____

Choose **FOUR** <u>necessary</u> things
that you can accomplish today.

My Dreams for Tomorrow:

_____
_____
_____

DAY 17

Date:_____

Choose **FOUR** <u>important</u> things
that you can accomplish today.

Reflect on Yesterday's Accomplishments:

_____
_____
_____

DAY 18

Date:_____

Choose **FOUR** <u>necessary</u> things that you can accomplish today.

My Dreams for Tomorrow:

_____
_____
_____

DAY 19

Date:_____

Choose **FOUR** <u>important</u> things
that you can accomplish today.

Reflect on Yesterday's Accomplishments:

_____

_____

_____

DAY 20

Choose **FOUR** <u>necessary</u> things that you can accomplish today.

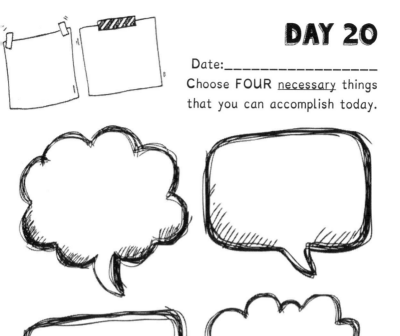

My Dreams for Tomorrow:

_____

_____

_____

DAY 21

Date:_____

Choose **FOUR** <u>important</u> things
that you can accomplish today.

Reflect on Yesterday's Accomplishments:

_____
_____
_____

DAY 22

Date:_____

Choose **FOUR** <u>necessary</u> things
that you can accomplish today.

My Dreams for Tomorrow:

_____
_____
_____

DAY 23

Date:_____

Choose **FOUR** <u>important</u> things
that you can accomplish today.

Reflect on Yesterday's Accomplishments:

_____
_____
_____

DAY 24

Choose **FOUR** <u>necessary</u> things that you can accomplish today.

My Dreams for Tomorrow:

_____
_____
_____

DAY 25

Date:_____

Choose **FOUR** <u>important</u> things that you can accomplish today.

Reflect on Yesterday's Accomplishments:

_____
_____
_____

DAY 26

Date:_____

Choose **FOUR** <u>necessary</u> things
that you can accomplish today.

My Dreams for Tomorrow:

_____
_____
_____

DAY 27

Date:_____

Choose **FOUR** <u>important</u> things
that you can accomplish today.

Reflect on Yesterday's Accomplishments:

_____
_____
_____

DAY 28

Date:_____

Choose **FOUR** <u>necessary</u> things that you can accomplish today.

My Dreams for Tomorrow:

_____
_____
_____

DAY 29

Date:_____

Choose **FOUR** <u>important</u> things
that you can accomplish today.

Reflect on Yesterday's Accomplishments:

_____

_____

_____

Date:_____

Choose **FOUR** <u>necessary</u> things that you can accomplish today.

My Dreams for Tomorrow:

_____

_____

_____

DAY 31

Date:_____

Choose **FOUR** <u>important</u> things
that you can accomplish today.

Reflect on Yesterday's Accomplishments:

_____
_____
_____

DAY 32

Choose **FOUR** <u>necessary</u> things
that you can accomplish today.

My Dreams for Tomorrow:

_____
_____
_____

DAY 33

Date:_____

Choose **FOUR** <u>important</u> things
that you can accomplish today.

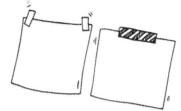

Reflect on Yesterday's Accomplishments:

_____
_____
_____

DAY 34

Date:_____

Choose **FOUR** <u>necessary</u> things
that you can accomplish today.

My Dreams for Tomorrow:

_____
_____
_____

DAY 35

Date:_____

Choose **FOUR** <u>important</u> things
that you can accomplish today.

Reflect on Yesterday's Accomplishments:

_____

_____

_____

DAY 36

Date:_____

Choose FOUR <u>necessary</u> things that you can accomplish today.

My Dreams for Tomorrow:

_____
_____
_____

DAY 37

Date:_____

Choose **FOUR** <u>important</u> things that you can accomplish today.

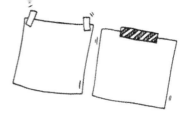

Reflect on Yesterday's Accomplishments:

_____
_____
_____

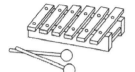

DAY 38

Date:_____

Choose FOUR <u>necessary</u> things
that you can accomplish today.

My Dreams for Tomorrow:

_____
_____
_____

DAY 39

Date:_____

Choose **FOUR** <u>important</u> things
that you can accomplish today.

Reflect on Yesterday's Accomplishments:

_____
_____
_____

Date:_____

Choose **FOUR** <u>necessary</u> things that you can accomplish today.

My Dreams for Tomorrow:

_____

_____

_____

DAY 41

Date:_____

Choose **FOUR** <u>important</u> things
that you can accomplish today.

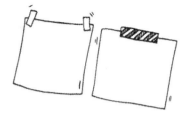

Reflect on Yesterday's Accomplishments:

_____
_____
_____

DAY 42

Date:_____

Choose **FOUR** <u>necessary</u> things
that you can accomplish today.

My Dreams for Tomorrow:

_____

_____

_____

DAY 43

Date:_____

Choose **FOUR** <u>important</u> things
that you can accomplish today.

Reflect on Yesterday's Accomplishments:

_____
_____
_____

DAY 44

Date:_____

Choose **FOUR** <u>necessary</u> things
that you can accomplish today.

My Dreams for Tomorrow:

_____
_____
_____

DAY 45

Date:_____

Choose **FOUR** <u>important</u> things
that you can accomplish today.

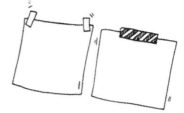

Reflect on Yesterday's Accomplishments:

_____
_____
_____

DAY 46

Date:_____

Choose **FOUR** <u>necessary</u> things that you can accomplish today.

My Dreams for Tomorrow:

_____
_____
_____

DAY 47

Date:_____

Choose **FOUR** <u>important</u> things
that you can accomplish today.

Reflect on Yesterday's Accomplishments:

_____
_____
_____

DAY 48

Date:_____

Choose **FOUR** <u>necessary</u> things that you can accomplish today.

My Dreams for Tomorrow:

_____
_____
_____

DAY 49

Date:_____

Choose **FOUR** <u>important</u> things
that you can accomplish today.

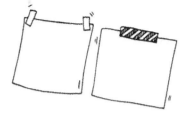

Reflect on Yesterday's Accomplishments:

_____
_____
_____

DAY 50

Date:_____

Choose **FOUR** <u>necessary</u> things
that you can accomplish today.

My Dreams for Tomorrow:

_____
_____
_____

DAY 51

Date:_____

Choose **FOUR** <u>important</u> things
that you can accomplish today.

Reflect on Yesterday's Accomplishments:

_____
_____
_____

DAY 52

Date:_____

Choose **FOUR** <u>necessary</u> things
that you can accomplish today.

My Dreams for Tomorrow:

_____
_____
_____

DAY 53

Date:_____

Choose **FOUR** <u>important</u> things
that you can accomplish today.

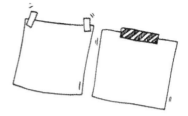

Reflect on Yesterday's Accomplishments:

_____
_____
_____

DAY 54

Date:_____

Choose **FOUR** <u>necessary</u> things
that you can accomplish today.

My Dreams for Tomorrow:

_____
_____
_____

DAY 55

Date:_____

Choose **FOUR** <u>important</u> things
that you can accomplish today.

Reflect on Yesterday's Accomplishments:

_____
_____
_____

DAY 56

Date:_____

Choose **FOUR** <u>necessary</u> things that you can accomplish today.

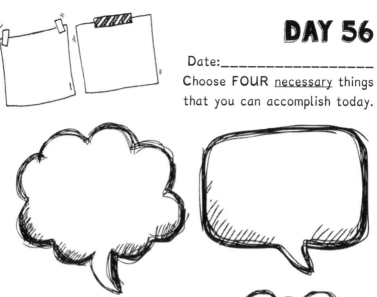

My Dreams for Tomorrow:

_____
_____
_____

DAY 57

Date:_____

Choose **FOUR** <u>important</u> things
that you can accomplish today.

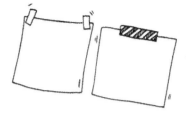

Reflect on Yesterday's Accomplishments:

_____
_____
_____

DAY 58

Date:_____

Choose **FOUR** <u>necessary</u> things that you can accomplish today.

My Dreams for Tomorrow:

DAY 59

Date:_____

Choose **FOUR** <u>important</u> things
that you can accomplish today.

Reflect on Yesterday's Accomplishments:

DAY 60

Choose **FOUR** <u>necessary</u> things
that you can accomplish today.

My Dreams for Tomorrow:

_____
_____
_____

DAY 61

Date:_____

Choose **FOUR** <u>important</u> things
that you can accomplish today.

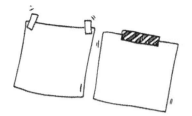

Reflect on Yesterday's Accomplishments:

_____
_____
_____

DAY 62

Date:_____

Choose **FOUR** <u>necessary</u> things that you can accomplish today.

My Dreams for Tomorrow:

_____
_____
_____

DAY 63

Date:_____

Choose **FOUR** <u>important</u> things
that you can accomplish today.

Reflect on Yesterday's Accomplishments:

_____
_____
_____

DAY 64

Date:_____

Choose **FOUR** <u>necessary</u> things that you can accomplish today.

My Dreams for Tomorrow:

_____
_____
_____

DAY 65

Date:_____

Choose **FOUR** <u>important</u> things
that you can accomplish today.

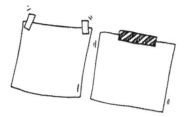

Reflect on Yesterday's Accomplishments:

_____
_____
_____

DAY 66

Date:_____

Choose **FOUR** <u>necessary</u> things
that you can accomplish today.

My Dreams for Tomorrow:

_____
_____
_____

DAY 67

Date:_____

Choose **FOUR** <u>important</u> things
that you can accomplish today.

Reflect on Yesterday's Accomplishments:

_____
_____
_____

DAY 68

Date:_____

Choose **FOUR** <u>necessary</u> things
that you can accomplish today.

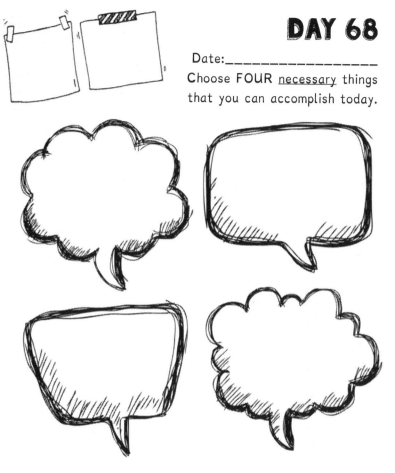

My Dreams for Tomorrow:

_____
_____
_____

DAY 69

Date:_____

Choose **FOUR** <u>important</u> things
that you can accomplish today.

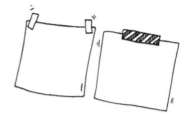

Reflect on Yesterday's Accomplishments:

_____
_____
_____

DAY 70

Date:_____

Choose **FOUR** <u>necessary</u> things
that you can accomplish today.

My Dreams for Tomorrow:

_____
_____
_____

DAY 71

Date:_____

Choose **FOUR** <u>important</u> things
that you can accomplish today.

Reflect on Yesterday's Accomplishments:

DAY 72

Date:_____

Choose **FOUR** <u>necessary</u> things
that you can accomplish today.

My Dreams for Tomorrow:

DAY 73

Date:_____

Choose **FOUR** <u>important</u> things
that you can accomplish today.

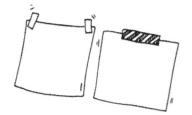

Reflect on Yesterday's Accomplishments:

DAY 74

Date:_____

Choose **FOUR** <u>necessary</u> things
that you can accomplish today.

My Dreams for Tomorrow:

_____
_____
_____

DAY 75

Date:_____
Choose **FOUR** <u>important</u> things
that you can accomplish today.

Reflect on Yesterday's Accomplishments:
_____
_____
_____

Date:_____

Choose **FOUR** <u>necessary</u> things that you can accomplish today.

My Dreams for Tomorrow:

_____
_____
_____

DAY 77

Date:_____

Choose **FOUR** <u>important</u> things
that you can accomplish today.

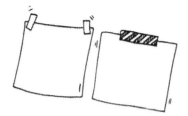

Reflect on Yesterday's Accomplishments:

_____

_____

_____

DAY 78

Date:_____

Choose **FOUR** <u>necessary</u> things
that you can accomplish today.

My Dreams for Tomorrow:

_____
_____
_____

DAY 79

Date:_____

Choose **FOUR** <u>important</u> things
that you can accomplish today.

Reflect on Yesterday's Accomplishments:

_____
_____
_____

DAY 80

Date:_____

Choose **FOUR** <u>necessary</u> things
that you can accomplish today.

My Dreams for Tomorrow:

DAY 81

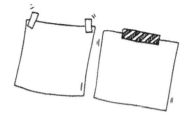

Date:_____

Choose **FOUR** <u>important</u> things
that you can accomplish today.

Reflect on Yesterday's Accomplishments:

DAY 82

Date:_____

Choose **FOUR** <u>necessary</u> things
that you can accomplish today.

My Dreams for Tomorrow:

_____
_____
_____

DAY 83

Date:_____

Choose **FOUR** <u>important</u> things
that you can accomplish today.

Reflect on Yesterday's Accomplishments:

_____

_____

_____

DAY 84

Choose **FOUR** <u>necessary</u> things
that you can accomplish today.

My Dreams for Tomorrow:

_____
_____
_____

DAY 85

Date:_____

Choose **FOUR** <u>important</u> things
that you can accomplish today.

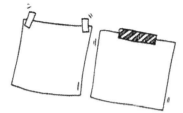

Reflect on Yesterday's Accomplishments:

DAY 86

Date:_____

Choose **FOUR** <u>necessary</u> things that you can accomplish today.

My Dreams for Tomorrow:

_____
_____
_____

DAY 87

Date:_____

Choose **FOUR** <u>important</u> things
that you can accomplish today.

Reflect on Yesterday's Accomplishments:

_____
_____
_____

DAY 88

Date:_____

Choose **FOUR** <u>necessary</u> things that you can accomplish today.

My Dreams for Tomorrow:

_____
_____
_____

DAY 89

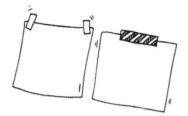

Date:_____

Choose **FOUR** <u>important</u> things
that you can accomplish today.

Reflect on Yesterday's Accomplishments:

_____
_____
_____

DAY 90

Date:_____

Choose **FOUR** <u>necessary</u> things
that you can accomplish today.

My Dreams for Tomorrow:

_____
_____
_____

My Notes:

My Notes:

Just for Fun

My Notes:

My Notes:

Just for Fun

My Notes:

Just for Fun

My Notes:

My Notes:

Just for Fun

My Notes:

My Notes:

Just for Fun

My Notes:

Just for Fun

My Notes:

SARAH'S SECRET:

Twelve Life Tips!

1. Don't make decisions based on your fears.
2. Don't gossip. "A whisperer separates the best of friends." People who gossip to you, will gossip about you.
3. Take advice from the people you want to be like. There will be people who try to control you, but do you want to end up like them?
4. Don't take advice from people who are driven by their fears. Take advice from those who live by faith and trust in God's word.
5. Don't be afraid to make mistakes, when they happen learn from them.
6. Overlook most of the drama that other people throw your way.
7. When in doubt, be gracious. Wisdom is knowing what to overlook.
8. Take a minute to encourage a child, no matter how busy you are.
9. Before you complain, remember the cross.
10. Enjoy today and love the people on your path, they are there for a reason.
11. If you have a dream, give it feet. What is the worst that could happen? God gave you that dream, don't waste it.
12. Dream big dreams, but take small steps. Little by little your life will be transformed.

Every Planner has a different Secret!